Understanding Dementia Training Workbook

For Health and Social Care Professionals Working in Adult Care Settings and Domiciliary Care

HSC Training Link

Copyright © 2016

All rights reserved.

ISBN-13: 978-1540888570
ISBN-10: 1540888576

ID# Index

1. Learning Outcomes
2. Candidate and Manager to complete
3. Learning Outcome 1 - Describe the common types of dementia
10. Learning Outcome 2 - Identify causes and symptoms of different types of dementia
19. Learning Outcome 3 - Understand brain structure and the different parts of the brain affected by dementia
26. Learning Outcome 4 - Understand how changes to the brain impact on how a person with dementia functions
36. References
37. Notes

Learning Outcomes

This training workbook will give you a general understanding of dementia; the diseases and conditions that can lead to dementia, the parts of the brain that are affected by dementia and how to recognise the wide range of symptoms.

Complete this workbook to demonstrate that you can:

1. Describe the common types of dementia

2. Identify causes and symptoms of different types of dementia

3. Understand brain structure and the different parts of the brain affected by dementia

4. Understand how changes to the brain impact on how a person with dementia functions

CANDIDATE DETAILS

Your name:

……………………………………………………………

Your signature

…………………………………………………………..

Place of employment:

……………………………………………………………

Date workbook started:

……………………………………………………………

Date workbook completed:

……………………………………………………………..

MANAGER DETAILS

I certify that the candidate named above completed this workbook.

Manager's name:

…………………………………………………………..

Manager's signature:

…………………………………………………………..

Date ……………………………………………………

LEARNING OUTCOME 1 - Describe the common types of dementia.

To understand dementia, you first need to know what it is and what it is not.

Definition of Dementia

"A chronic or persistent disorder of the mental processes caused by brain disease or injury and marked by memory disorders, personality changes, and impaired reasoning."

"Dementia is an umbrella term. It describes the symptoms that occur when the brain is affected by certain diseases or conditions. ... They are often named according to the condition that has caused the dementia."

(https://www.alzheimers.org.uk/typesofdementia)

Origin

"Late 18th century: from Latin, from demens, dement- out of one's mind."

(https://en.oxforddictionaries.com/definition/dementia)

How is Dementia Viewed?

Symptoms of dementia are accepted differently in different parts of the world. This includes considering dementia as a normal part of ageing, mental illness, something metaphysical linked to supernatural or spiritual beliefs or as an irreversible disease of the brain.

Low levels of understanding about dementia lead to various misconceptions.
We are also exposed to messages and information about dementia in our everyday lives through the media (newspapers, television, radio, magazines and the Internet).

As a result, the average person may make a judgement on what they think dementia is, based on what they have read or heard.

The actual word 'dementia', because of its Latin origins, can generally negatively affect how it is viewed.

In the world of medicine, Dementia is viewed differently. The word dementia is used to describe conditions that result in the progressive loss of mental ability, which affects the person's ability to remember, learn, understand, communicate and reason. There are also often changes in behaviour and a gradual loss of skills needed to carry out ordinary daily activities.

TASK 1

If someone was to ask you what dementia is, what would you say to him or her?

TASK 2

If someone who you suspected might have dementia asked you what dementia is, what would you say to him or her? If you would explain it differently, why?

'Living Well with Dementia' is the UK government's plan for improving health and social care services in England for everyone with dementia; to develop services that meet the needs of everyone, regardless of their age, ethnic group or social status.

One of the three 'key steps' to improve the quality of life for people with dementia is to ensure better knowledge about dementia and to remove stigma *(Living Well with Dementia: A National Dementia Strategy.)*

It is essential to know and understand that dementia must never be used as a label. We are all individual human beings and retain our humanness irrespective of any diagnosis given by a medical professional. Words such as 'senile' are neither appropriate nor acceptable and should be challenged at every opportunity.

Facts about Dementia

- There are 850,000 people with dementia in the UK, with numbers set to rise to over 1 million by 2025;
- It is estimated that 42,325 people have been diagnosed with young onset dementia, representing around 5% of the total people living with dementia;
- 1 in 6 people over the age of 80 have dementia;
- 70 per cent of people in care homes have dementia or severe memory problems;
- Dementia is one of the main causes of disability later in life, with higher statistics than cancer, cardiovascular disease and stroke;
- Dementia is the name given to a group of symptoms that characterise diseases and conditions of the brain. The most common form being 'Alzheimer's disease';
- Dementia is not necessarily part of the normal ageing process;
- Currently, there is no cure for dementia. Various treatments can help with the symptoms, especially in the early stages of Alzheimer's disease;
- Dementia is not an infectious disease.

Types of Dementia

As already mentioned, Alzheimer's disease is the most common form of dementia, but there are many others. It is very difficult to diagnose a specific type of dementia and most decisions on diagnosis are based on tests, medical history and observations of symptoms.

Alzheimers Disease

Alzheimer's disease is a physical disease that affects the entire brain. It affects around 62% of all people diagnosed with dementia. It is a slow disease, although how fast the changes occur vary from person to person. A person with Alzheimer's usually lives for 8 to 10 years after diagnosis. The brain cells deteriorate, resulting in the loss of cognitive functions. The brain of a person with Alzheimer's disease looks very different to other types of dementia. There are abnormal fibres and patches of degenerative nerve endings. This and a reduction in brain chemicals means that affected brain cells cannot communicate with each other. There is loss of cognitive functions such as memory, judgment, reasoning, movement, coordination and pattern recognition. The early stages reveal memory loss, mood swings and difficulties finding the correct words. As the disease progresses, there will be more confusion, increased mood swings, increased anger and sadness. People living with Alzheimer's may also feel very scared or frustrated, losing confidence and interest in life. The decline in functions is usually steadier than with other types of dementia.

Vascular Dementia

This type of dementia affects around 25% of people diagnosed with dementia. Around 25% of people who have Alzheimer's disease also have vascular dementia. The brain of a person with vascular dementia shows areas where brain cells have died through lack of oxygen. Oxygen is supplied to the brain via blood cells called the vascular system. If this system is diseased, or if a blockage occurs, blood cannot reach all parts of the brain. People with vascular dementia will experience memory loss and difficulties in communicating in the early stages. As the disease progresses, there will also be a loss of physical abilities. Vascular dementia does not affect the entire brain, so some abilities will remain. The decline in functions can appear quite suddenly. Because only part of the brain is affected, some people with vascular dementia will understand what is happening to them and so they could be affected by depression, frustration or display aggressive behaviour.

татк 3

How would you describe the main differences between Alzheimer's disease and vascular dementia?

Dementia with Lewy Bodies (DLB)

This is the third most common form of dementia and often starts rapidly or acutely. There can be quite a fast decline in the first few months, followed a levelling off. The course of the disease is usually five to seven years. A correct diagnosis is vital as oversensitivity to some dementia prescribed drugs can result in problems. DLB is caused by microscopic protein deposits in the brain, resulting in damage to nerve cells. The common symptoms of all types of dementia are experienced but there are also specific symptoms. In particular, people with DLB may experience periods where memory function is normal and there is no confusion. Impaired mental ability will fluctuate, with periods of normal function. In addition, 90% of people experience hallucinations – usually visual but sometimes auditory and most people retain an understanding that the hallucinations are not real. DLB can sometimes be confused with Parkinson's disease as other symptoms are similar – stiffness and rigidity, slow movement and tremor for example. There is also a disturbed sleep pattern with DLB.

Parkinson's Disease

Parkinson's disease is a degenerative disease of the nervous system, caused by the progressive loss of brain cells in the midbrain. People with Parkinson's disease display trembling arms and legs, muscle stiffness and rigidity and slow movement.

TASK 4

> How would you describe the main differences between DLB and Parkinson's disease?

TASK 5

Describe the common types of dementia:

LEARNING OUTCOME 2 - Identify causes and symptoms of different types of dementia.

You have now learned that 'dementia' is the umbrella term for a number of neurological conditions, of which the major symptom includes a largescale decline in brain function.

Dementia was a relatively rare occurrence before the 20th century as fewer people lived to old age in pre-industrial society. It was not until the mid-1970's that dementia began to be described as we know it today.

Over 100 diseases may cause dementia. The most common causes of dementia include *Alzheimer's disease*, *vascular dementia* and *dementia with Lewy bodies*. Other causes can be *genetic* or *environmental*.

How is Dementia Caused?

Dementia is caused by damage to the cells in the brain, so that they die faster than normal.

This damage could be the result of:

- Imbalance in the chemical messengers in the brain, causing the brain to shrink;

- Lack of blood (which carries oxygen) to parts of the brain;
- Pressure on the brain (a tumour for example);
- Infection (AIDS for example).

Genetic Causes

Some diseases are caused by a genetic mutation, or permanent change in one or more specific genes. If a person inherits from a parent a genetic mutation that causes a certain disease, then he or she will usually get the disease. Sickle cell anaemia, cystic fibrosis, and early-onset familial Alzheimer's disease are examples of inherited genetic disorders.
Where there are genetic causes, this means that there has been no illness or disease, nor any environmental factor. The most common genetic condition that can lead to dementia is *Down's syndrome*.

There are two types of Alzheimer's—early-onset and late-onset. Both types have a genetic component

Early-Onset Alzheimer's Disease

Early-onset Alzheimer's disease occurs in people age 30 to 60 and represents less than 5 per cent of all people with Alzheimer's. Most cases are caused by an inherited change in one of three genes, resulting in a type known as *early-onset familial Alzheimer's disease*, or FAD. For others, the disease appears to develop without any specific, known cause.

Late-Onset Alzheimer's Disease

Most people with Alzheimer's have the late-onset form of the disease, in which symptoms become apparent in the mid-60's and later. The causes of late-onset Alzheimer's are not yet completely understood, but they likely include a combination of genetic, environmental, and lifestyle factors that affect a person's risk for developing the disease.

The *gene flow* is the passing on of genes to future generations - this is called hereditary genetics. With regard to dementia from the gene flow, there are other specific conditions that can lead to dementia that *have* passed through the family genetic system. These include Huntington's disease and Parkinson's disease.

Environmental Causes

When we talk about environmental factors, we mean the surroundings that influence the development and growth of people and the effects that pollution or outside influences have on a person's health. Environmental research is ongoing and new influences are being studied all the time. What we so far know is that possible causes for dementia include things like toxic emissions, smoking and excess alcohol. Some studies of industrialised areas have found that the ratio of people diagnosed with a dementia is higher than in non-industrialised areas.

Alcohol

Excessive alcohol has a harmful effect on the nerve cells in the outer brain, affecting a wide range of abilities. This is called *alcoholic dementia* or *Korsakoff's syndrome,* caused by a lack of thiamine (Vitamin B1). This could be due to poor nutrition (or poor absorption of vitamins due to the effect of alcohol on the stomach lining.

Head Injuries/ Pressure on the Brain

People with severe head injuries are considered to be at higher risk of developing dementia.

TASK 6

From what you have learned so far in this workbook, describe the causes of dementia:

We briefly looked at *Alzheimer's disease* (the progressive loss of nerve cells without known cause) and *vascular dementia* (i.e. loss of brain function due to a series of small strokes) earlier. These are the two major degenerative causes of dementia.

Alzheimer's Disease

We have briefly looked at how this disease is caused by abnormal deposits of protein in the brain that destroy cells in the areas of the brain that control memory and mental functions.
These protein deposits accumulate gradually and progressively. Only when brain cell loss progresses and a certain threshold is reached do the clinical symptoms of Alzheimer's disease start to appear. It can take between 10 and 20 years before obvious signs of the disease are seen.

There are two known *risk factors* for developing the disease:

1. Advancing age: About 5% of people over 65 years of age, 20% of those over 80 years and 30% of those over 90 have the disease.

2. Family history: Genetics were mentioned earlier. Statistically, people who have a parent or sibling affected by AD are two to three times more likely to develop the disease than those with no family history. If the disease has affected more than one close relative, the risk increases even more.

Vascular Dementia

This dementia is caused by *atherosclerosis*, caused by (for example) deposits of fats, dead cells and other debris that form on the inside of arteries and partially (or completely) block blood flow. These blockages may cause multiple strokes, or interruptions of blood flow, to the brain. Because this interruption of blood flow is also called 'infarction', this type of dementia is sometimes called multi-infarct dementia. Vascular dementia is often related to high blood pressure, high cholesterol, heart disease, diabetes, and related conditions. Treating those conditions can slow down the progress of vascular dementia, but functions are not recovered once they are lost. Vascular dementia may occur at the same time as Alzheimer's disease, resulting in a condition called *Mixed Dementia*.

Other irreversible medical conditions that can cause dementia (at a much lower rate) include Parkinson's disease, Huntington's disease, Pick's disease, or Creutzfeldt-Jakob disease.

TASK 7 – QUESTIONS AND ANSWERS

1. Dementia is a mental illness.	Yes/No
2. There are over 100 diseases that can cause dementia.	Yes/No
3. Dementia can be caused by lifestyle.	Yes/No
4. Alzheimer's and dementia are the same thing.	Yes/No
5. Dementia is caused by damage to the cells in the brain.	Yes/No
6. Your age raises your risk of Alzheimer's.	Yes/No
7. Dementia is not a progressive illness.	Yes/No
8. Dementia is a normal part of ageing.	Yes/No
9. Alzheimer's disease can resemble the early stages of Parkinson's disease.	Yes/No
10. Dementia is diagnosed by a blood test.	Yes/No

Symptoms

Alzheimer's Disease

As the earliest signs resemble natural ageing, they may be overlooked. Mild impairment in thinking is the most significant sign of the early stage. Other symptoms include:

- Unexplained weight loss
- Motor problems (including mild walking difficulties)
- Forgetfulness
- Loss of concentration

It is worth noting that in people who do not have Alzheimer's disease, all of the symptoms can be the result of fatigue, grief/depression, illness, sensory loss, medication/alcohol.

The brain degeneration that occurs in Alzheimer's disease affects memory, thinking skills, emotions, behaviour and mood. Alzheimer's disease typically starts slowly and in the early stages, the symptoms can be very subtle.

However, as the disease progresses, symptoms become more noticeable and interfere with daily life.
The disease affects each person differently and the symptoms experienced vary. Common symptoms may include:

- Persistent and frequent memory loss, especially of recent events
- Vagueness in everyday conversation
- Being less able to plan, problem solve, organise and think logically
- Language difficulties such as finding the right word and understanding conversations
- Apparent loss of enthusiasm for previously enjoyed activities
- Taking longer to do routine tasks
- Becoming disoriented, even in well-known places

- Inability to process questions and instructions
- Deterioration of social skills
- Emotional unpredictability
- Changes in behaviour, personality and mood

Symptoms vary over time as the disease progresses and different areas of the brain are affected. A person's abilities may fluctuate from day-to-day, or even within the one day, and can become worse in times of stress, fatigue or ill health.

Vascular Dementia

We have learned that vascular dementia is a general term describing problems with reasoning, planning, judgement, memory and other thinking skills that are significant enough to interfere with daily social or occupational functioning, and is caused by brain damage that has resulted from impaired blood flow in the brain.

Vascular dementia can sometimes develop after a stroke blocks an artery in the brain, but strokes do not always cause vascular dementia. Whether a stroke affects thinking and reasoning depends on the severity and location of the stroke.

Vascular dementia more often results from many small strokes or other conditions that damage blood vessels and reduce circulation, reducing the supply of vital oxygen and nutrients to brain cells.

In Alzheimer's disease, memory problems (especially forgetting recent events), is often the most prominent symptom. In vascular dementia however, executive functions (planning, reasoning, judgement), spatial processing and attention are often more impaired.

Pure vascular dementia is not common. Often, vascular damage occurs alongside Alzheimer's disease or other brain disease and exacerbates the dementia, rather than being the primary cause.

One single large stroke can sometimes cause vascular dementia depending on the size and location of the stroke. This type of vascular dementia, called strategic infarct dementia, is characterised by the sudden onset of changes in thinking skills or behaviour after a stroke. The symptoms depend on the location of the stroke and what brain functions are affected by the damage. Provided no further strokes occur, the person's symptoms may remain stable or even get better over time. However, if there is other vascular disease also affecting the brain or additional strokes occur, symptoms may get worse.

One form of vascular dementia is called multi-infarct dementia and is caused by multiple strokes. This is associated with disease of the brain's large blood vessels. The strokes are often silent, that is the person does not notice any symptoms when they occur. Over time, as more strokes occur, more damage is done to the brain and reasoning and thinking skills may be affected to the point that a diagnosis of vascular dementia is made. Other symptoms can include depression and mood swings, but the symptoms very much depend on the location of the brain damage. Multi-infarct dementia can have a step-wise progression, where symptoms worsen after a new stroke, then stabilise for a time.

Another form of vascular dementia is called subcortical dementia, or sometimes Binswanger's disease. This is associated with disease in the small blood vessels deep within the brain and damage to deep (subcortical) areas of the brain. It can be a consequence of untreated high blood pressure or diabetes leading to vascular disease. Symptoms often include deterioration of reasoning and thinking skills, mild memory problems, walking and movement problems, behavioural changes and lack of bladder control. Subcortical vascular dementia is usually progressive, with symptoms getting worse over time as more vascular damage occurs, although people's abilities fluctuate.

TASK 8

Describe the more common symptoms of dementia:

AGEING AND DEMENTIA	
Early Signs	
NORMAL AGEING	**DEMENTIA**
Memory and Concentration	
<ul><li>Periodic minor memory lapses or forgetfulness of part of an experience</li><li>Occasional lapses in attention or concentration</li></ul>	<ul><li>Important items misplaced</li><li>Confused/ upset if cannot perform simple tasks</li><li>Trouble with simple arithmetical problems</li><li>Difficulty making routine decisions</li><li>Confusion about month or season</li><li>Loss of short-term memory</li></ul>
Mood and Behaviour	
<ul><li>Temporary sadness or anxiety, based on appropriate and specific causes</li><li>Changing interests</li><li>Increasingly cautious behaviour</li></ul>	<ul><li>Unpredictable mood changes</li><li>Changes in personality/behaviour</li><li>Increasing loss of interest in people or activities</li><li>Depression/ anger/confusion in response to change</li><li>Denial of symptoms</li></ul>
Progressive Signs	
Language and Speech	
<ul><li>Unimpaired language skills</li></ul>	<ul><li>Difficulty completing sentences or finding the right words</li><li>Inability to understand word meanings</li><li>More likely to keep repeating themselves</li><li>Reduced and/or irrelevant conversation</li></ul>
Memory	
<ul><li>Slight lapses in remembering names or faces</li></ul>	<ul><li>Visual memory loss – no recognition of a relative</li><li>Long-term memory loss – forgets childhood/ family members</li><li>Emotional – unable to show emotion towards family</li></ul>
Movement and Coordination	
<ul><li>Increasingly cautious in movement</li><li>Slower reaction times</li></ul>	<ul><li>Visibly impaired movement/ coordination, slowing of movements, halting gait. reduced sense of balance</li><li>Problems with spatial and temporal orientation</li></ul>
Other Symptoms	
<ul><li>Normal sense of smell</li><li>No abnormal weight changes</li></ul>	<ul><li>Impaired sense of smell</li><li>Severe weight loss</li></ul>

LEARNING OUTCOME 3 - Understand brain structure and the different parts of the brain affected by dementia.

The brain performs many vital functions. It gives meaning to things that happen in the world around us.

We have five senses:

- Sight
- Smell
- Taste
- Hearing
- Touch

The brain receives messages through these senses. Because the brain is such a complex organ, it is able to receive many messages at the same time. It is an organised organ, divided into many parts, each serving specific functions.

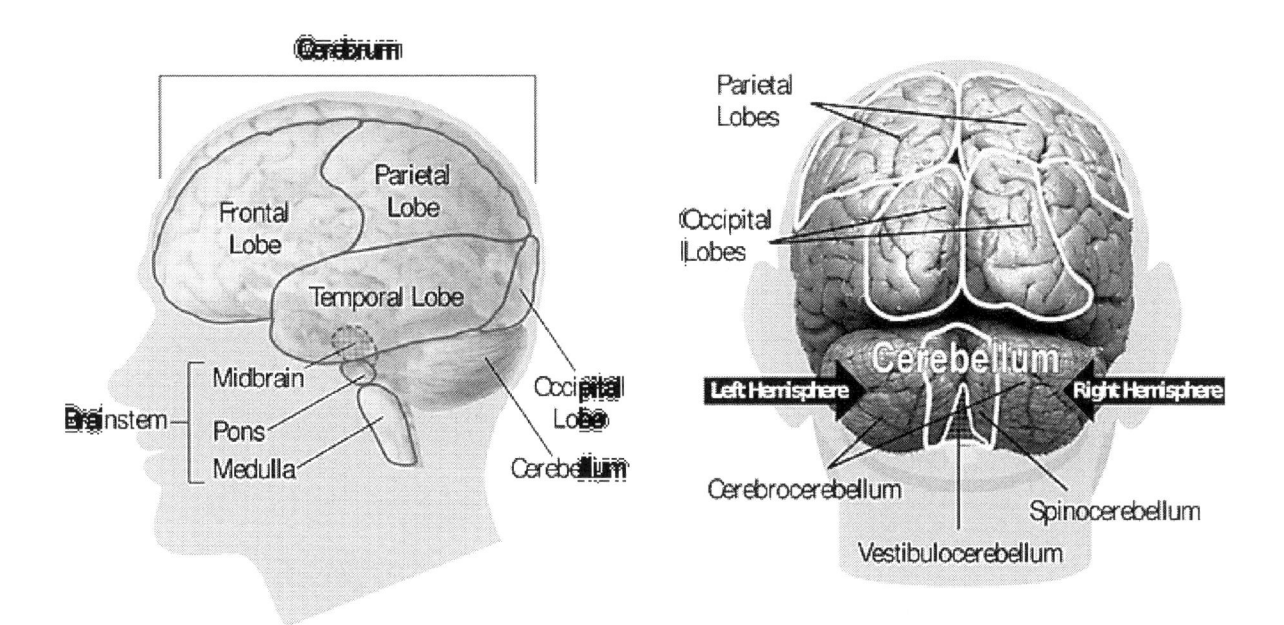

Parts of the Brain

The *Cerebrum* is the largest part of the brain. Higher brain functions take place in the surface of the cerebrum (neocortex). The neocortex is approximately 1.5 to 4 millimetres thick. It is dense with *neurons* – about 25 billion of them.

Cerebellum

This is the second largest part of the brain. It is made up of two hemispheres and it can be divided in to 5 lobes. Each lobe is responsible for different functions. It is connected to the brainstem and is the centre for body movement and balance.

Neurons

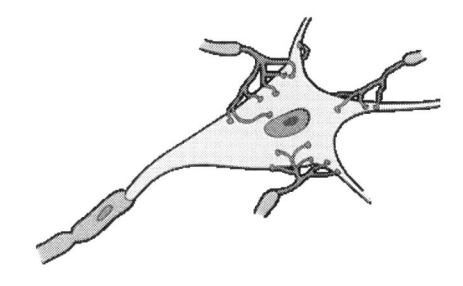

A neuron is a nerve cell, the basic building block of the nervous system. Neurons are similar to other cells in the human body, but there is one key difference between neurons and other cells. Neurons are specialised to transmit information throughout the body.

Neurons are responsible for communicating information in both chemical and electrical forms. Sensory neurons carry information from the sensory receptor cells throughout the body to the brain. Motor neurons transmit information from the brain to the muscles of the body. Interneurons are responsible for communicating information between different neurons in the body.

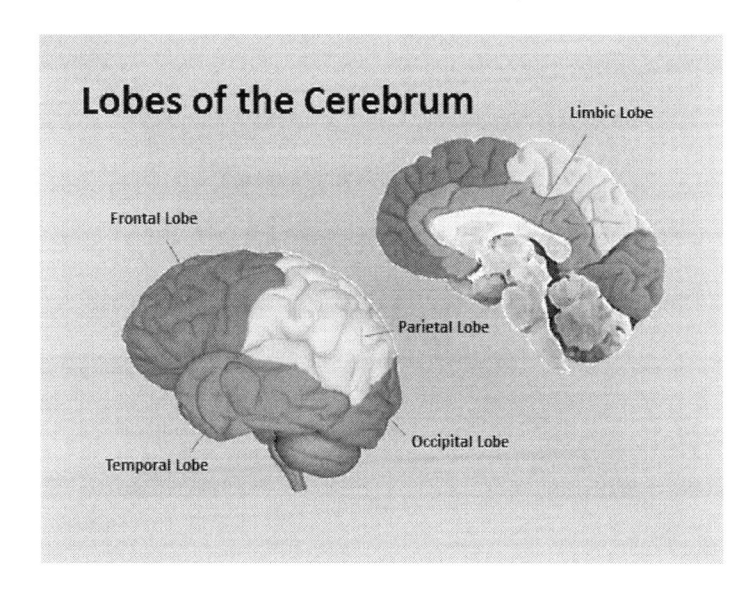

Lobes of the Cerebrum

The areas affected by dementia are:

- Frontal lobes
- Temporal lobes
- Parietal lobes

Frontal Lobes

These lobes are found at the front of the brain and have different parts to them:

- Motor cortex
- Pre-motor cortex

- Prefrontal cortex
- Broca's area

The frontal lobes are responsible for:

- Problem solving
- Spontaneity
- Memory
- Language
- Motivation
- Judgment
- Impulse control
- Social and sexual behaviour

Motor Cortex

This produces impulses that control the act of movement. The motor cortex is therefore involved in virtually everything we do – from gesturing, to talking, smiling, walking etc.

Pre-Motor Cortex

This part of the brain is involved in the sensory guidance of movement and controls the muscles of the trunk and proximal muscles (midriff).

Prefrontal Cortex

This plays an important part in memory, intelligence, concentration, temper and personality and our emotional characteristics. It helps us to set goals, make plans, judge and organise our priorities.

Broca's Area

This plays a part in language production,

Temporal Lobes

- Plays a role in emotions

- Responsible for smell, taste, perception, memory, understanding music, aggressiveness, sexual behaviour
- Contains a language and speech area, memory storage unit and primary auditory (hearing) cortex

Parietal Lobes

- Plays a role in touch, smell, taste
- Processes sensory and spatial awareness
- A key component in eye-hand co-ordination/arm movement
- Contains Wernicke's area
- Responsible for matching written words with the sound of spoken speech

Occipital Lobe

This part of the brain controls vision and recognition.

Limbic Lobe

The limbic lobe is found deep in the brain and makes up the limbic system. It regulates emotion and memory, directly connecting the lower and higher brain functions.

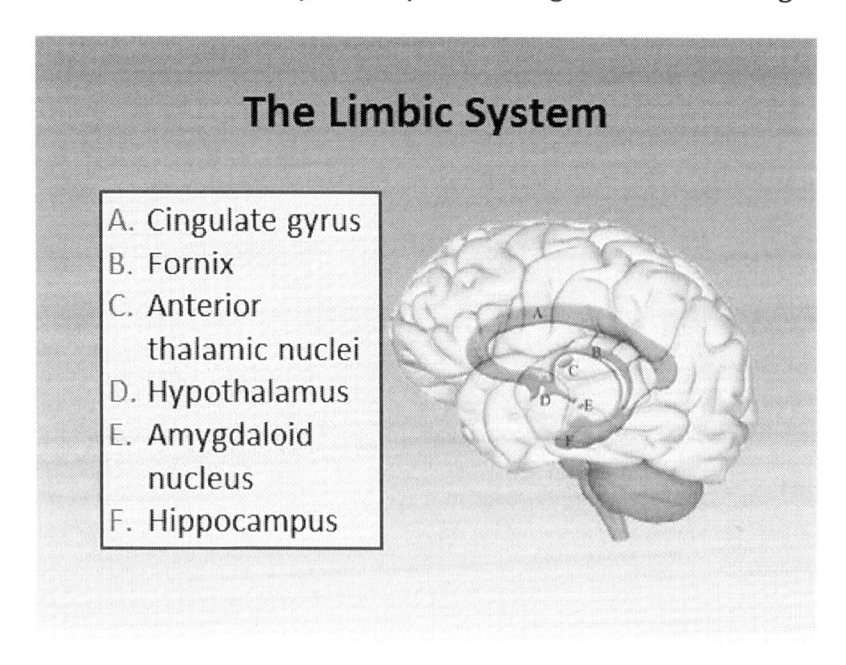

The Limbic System

A. Cingulate gyrus
B. Fornix
C. Anterior thalamic nuclei
D. Hypothalamus
E. Amygdaloid nucleus
F. Hippocampus

Thalamus

- This sits deep in the brain at the **top** of the **brainstem**
  - The **gateway** to the cerebral cortex
- ☑ Nearly all **sensory inputs** pass through it to the higher levels of the brain

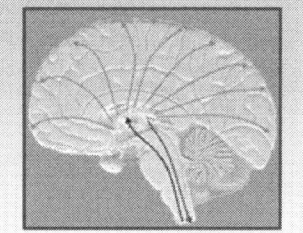

Hypothalamus

- Located under the thalamus and controls autonomic nervous system
- Centre for emotional response and behaviour
- Regulates body temperature/food intake, water balance and thirst
- Controls sleep-wake cycles/endocrine system

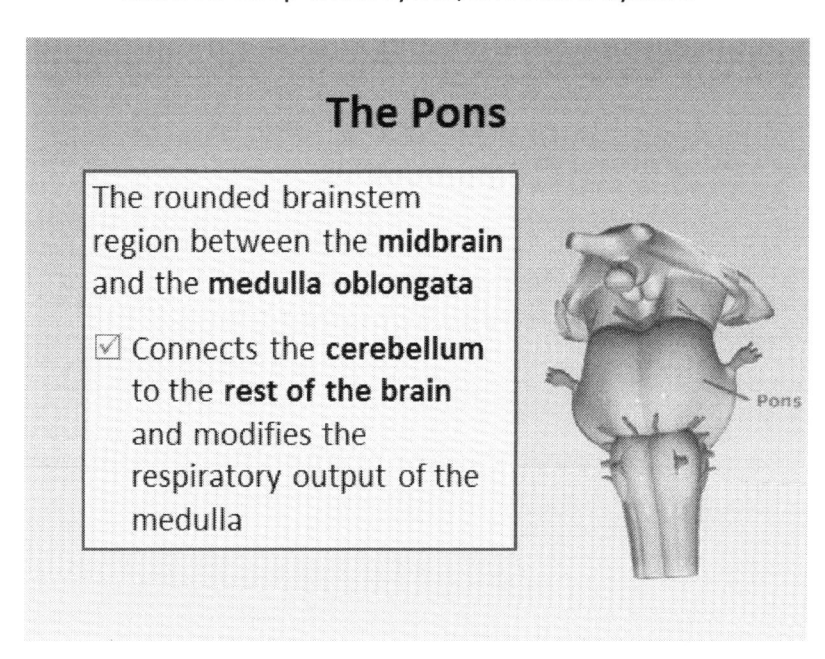

The Pons

The rounded brainstem region between the **midbrain** and the **medulla oblongata**

☑ Connects the **cerebellum** to the **rest of the brain** and modifies the respiratory output of the medulla

Ventricles

These are a complex series of spaces and tunnels through the centre of the brain. The ventricles secrete cerebrospinal fluid (which suspends the brain in the skull). They provide a route for chemical messengers that are widely distributed through the central nervous system.

Cerebrospinal Fluid

- A colourless liquid that bathes the brain and spine
- Formed within the ventricles of the brain
- Circulates throughout the central nervous system
- Fills the ventricles and meninges allowing the brain to 'float' within the skull

Brainstem

This is the most primitive part of the brain - but it controls the basic functions of life:

- Breathing, heart rate, swallowing, reflexes to sight or sound, sweating, blood pressure, sleep, and balance

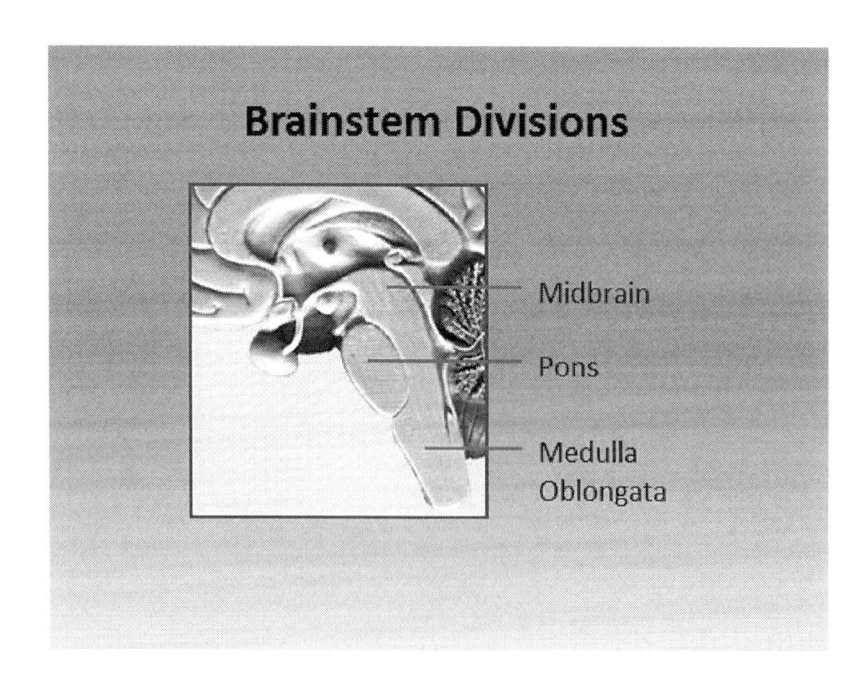

Brainstem Divisions
- Midbrain
- Pons
- Medulla Oblongata

TASK 9 - Label these parts of the brain:

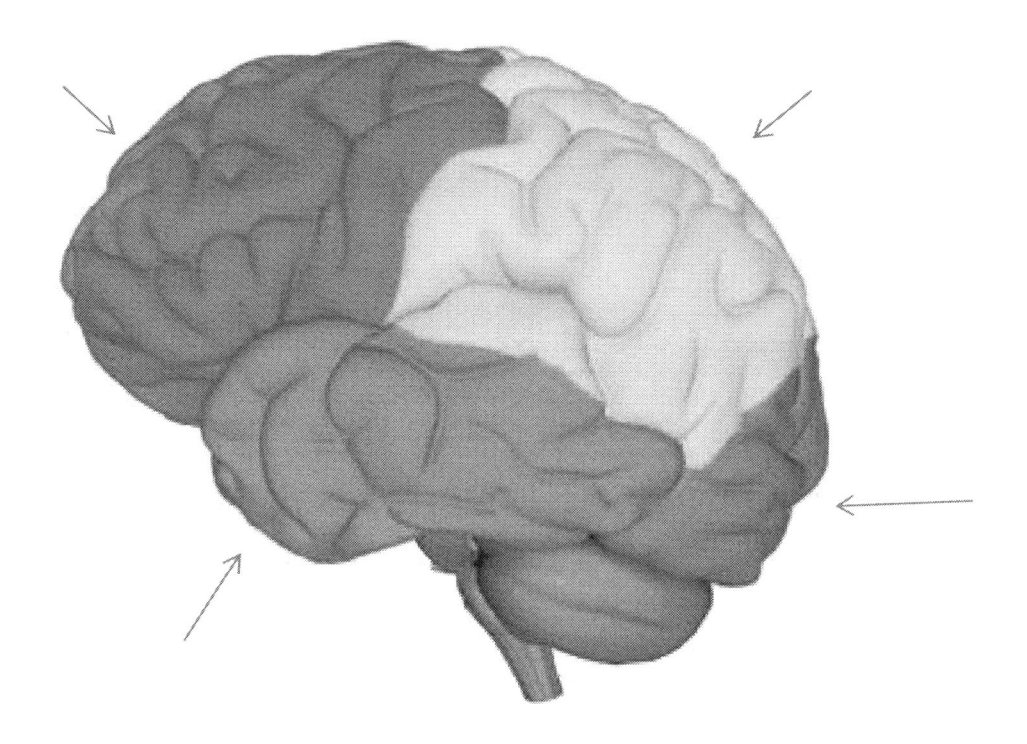

TASK 10

In your own words, describe how the brain is structured:

LEARNING OUTCOME 4 - Understand how changes to the brain impact on how a person with dementia functions

As mentioned, the three parts of the brain affected by dementia are the frontal, parietal and temporal lobes. The frontal lobes contain the *motor cortex*, the *pre-motor cortex*, the *prefrontal cortex* and *Broca's area*. The *motor* and *pre-motor cortex*'s play a vital role in *movement*.

Movement of the body includes:

- The contraction of muscles
- Movement in the direction required
- Movement of the correct muscles
- How much effort/force is required to move

How well the body moves is also affected by how the brain has interpreted the environment.

An example: *Reaching out to pour water from a jug*

The brain needs to calculate:

- Which muscles to use and in the correct order
- How to use those muscles to direct the hand and arm towards the jug
- Environmental factors to calculate:

- How much effort is needed to pick the jug up
- How heavy the jug is?
- How much water does it contain?
- What is the jug made from?

Dementia in any motor cortex affects coordination, intended voluntary movements, walking, pointing, gesturing etc.

In the previous example, the *pre-motor cortex* would help in the positioning of the body before reaching for the jug of water.

Where there is damage from dementia to the *pre-frontal cortex* behaviours could include:

- Behavioural disorders
- Lack of inhibition
- Lack of capacity to concentrate
- Recent memory impairment
- Inattentiveness

Broca's area is one of the areas significant to language production; speech is affected if dementia damages Broca's Area. Broca's area coordinates the muscles of the lips, tongue, jaw, and vocal cords to produce understandable speech.

Temporal Lobe

This part of the brain plays a role in emotion, smell, taste, perception, memory, understanding music, aggressiveness and sexual behaviour.

It also contains a language and speech area, memory storage unit and the primary auditory (hearing) cortex.

Temporal lobe damage from dementia results in:

- Language difficulties
- Inability to find the right words (aphasia)
- Reading difficulties
- Loss of recognition of familiar voices
- Difficulty in interpreting facial expression
- Loss of ability to recognise the meaning of tones - e.g. happiness, irritation
- Social skills are also affected

The importance of the auditory function:

- Hearing sounds
- Giving meaning to sounds (in dementia, hearing a noise but not understanding what it means – e.g. fire alarm)
- Puts sounds to words that are read

The temporal lobe also houses the 'memory storage unit'. This holds information about the past and knowledge. It contains experiences and memories, all of which make a person 'who they are'.

- Recognising faces, names and places can all be affected

Parietal Lobes

We have already discussed that this part of the brain plays a role in touch, smell and taste. Sensory and spatial awareness is also processed here. These lobes are also a key component of eye-hand co-ordination/arm movement. *Wernicke's area* is found in this part of the brain – which is responsible for matching written words with the sound of spoken speech.

Processed simultaneously:

- Sensory signals received from other areas in the brain
- Vision, hearing, motor functions, senses and memory
- Memory and new information received give meaning to objects

Example of how this works: an object that has feathers and two wings walks past. The senses of vision and memory tell the brain that this is a bird. If it quacks, the senses and memory tell you that this is a duck. If it clucks, it is a chicken.

Processes information about:

- Temperature
- Taste and touch
- Movement coming from the rest of the body
- Reading and mathematical problems
- Coordination

The lobes also enable us to know our left from our right and where each limb is in relation to the others.

Dementia in this area results in:

- An inability to distinguish between sensory stimuli - a person may smell coffee but thinks it is tea
- Body disorientation - in relation to the environment around them, or inability to locate or recognise parts of the body, resulting in problems with washing and dressing – which can lead to self-neglect

Dementia in this area can also result in:

- Inability to write
- Inability to read
- Inability to carry out very simple mathematical tasks (e.g. 3 + 3 =6)

TASK 11

In your care setting, there is a client called David, who has a type of dementia that affects his frontal lobes. Describe how this might affect him.

TASK 12

Thinking again about David . . . as a care worker, what challenges might you face?

TASK 13

In your care setting, there is a client called Maria, who has a type of dementia that affects her temporal lobes. Describe how this might affect her.

TASK 14

Thinking again about Maria . . . as a care worker, what challenges might you face?

TASK 15

In your care setting, there is a client called Maurice, who has a type of dementia that affects his parietal lobes. Describe how this might affect him.

TASK 16

Thinking again about Maurice . . . as a care worker, what challenges might you face?

TASK 17 Answer the following questions as simply as possible:

If someone asked you how brain cells are damaged in a person with dementia – what would you say?

If someone asked you why a person with dementia can do several things perfectly well, but not other things, what would you say?

Why is the temporal lobe important?

Why is the parietal lobe important?

The brain receives messages from five senses - what are they?

Three main areas of the brain are affected by dementia – what are they?

References

Adams, T., Manthorpe, J. – Dementia Care: An Evidence Based Textbook. Hodder Arnold. London

Alzheimer's Society

Common Core Principles for Supporting People with Dementia. A guide to training the social care and health workforce. Karen Davies, Skills for Health .James Cross, Skills for Care.

Oxford Dictionary (https://en.oxforddictionaries.com/definition/dementia).

The Human Brain: An Introduction to Its Functional Anatomy, Fifth Edition. Nolte, Mosby.

UK Government - Living Well with Dementia: A National Dementia Strategy.

NOTES

NOTES

NOTES

NOTES

NOTES

NOTES

Printed in Great Britain
by Amazon